PLAY TO YOUR STRENGTHS:

Games for Leaders and Teams

Faith Ralston, Ph. D.

ISBN: 0972787569 (sc)
ISBN: 0972787577 (e)

Because of the dynamic nature of the Internet, any web addresses or links contained in this book may have changed since publication and may no longer be valid. The views expressed in this work are solely those of the author and do not necessarily reflect the views of the publisher, and the publisher hereby disclaims any responsibility for them.

Any people depicted in stock imagery provided by Thinkstock are models, and such images are being used for illustrative purposes only.
Certain stock imagery © Thinkstock.

Play to Your Strengths Consulting
24 Duck Pass, North Oaks, MN 55127
6127015689

rev. date: 03/29/2016

A Note from Faith

Twelve years ago, I volunteered to lead a pilot workshop called "Discover Your Talents." It was scheduled for a Friday morning, at 7:30 a.m., in a small, remote conference room.

A few days before the program, the coordinator called in a panic. She exclaimed, "There are 450 people signed up for your workshop—including the CEO!"

Such an overwhelming response certainly got my attention.

Since that time, I've been on a mission to help others discover their talents. My mother used to say, "Faith, you only need to do one thing well, and the rest will fall into place." Her advice was golden.

In school, I struggled until I started a Master's degree in counseling psychology; there, I found my sweet spot. From that moment, my education and career took off. Today, I work happily and productively in my talent zone.

Research tells us that 78% of employees aren't fully engaged at work. You have the power to change this. Help employees focus on their talents, and you'll see engagement and performance soar. It happens every time. I created *Play to Your Strengths* games to help you focus on strengths and achieve great things together.

Faith

Contents

Why Games?

Leaders, are you leading a team and striving to achieve results?
If so, you want everyone to be engaged and committed.

In my 30 years' experience working with teams, I've discovered it's the simple things that cause problems—like getting to know each other, clarifying roles, and communicating expectations.

Whether you're currently leading a team or starting a new one, *Play to Your Strengths* games will help you engage everyone and gain real commitment. With these tools, you'll be able to make better decisions, talk openly, agree on priorities, and build greater trust.

I have used these games successfully with hundreds of teams. Now I'm putting these valuable tools in your hands. *Play to Your Strengths* games will transform your team into a powerhouse of performance—and you'll have fun using them. I look forward to hearing about your progress and seeing the results.

Please contact me at faith@faithralston.com to share your experiences!

Start playing today!
Order Play to Your Strengths© card packs
for your team or group event.
www.FaithRalston.com

Focus on Strengths!

Leaders, are you struggling to do more with less? If so, the answer may be in front of you. Research tells us *only 18%* of employees are engaged and committed to their jobs! This means you have 82% more resources available; you simply have to tap into them.

In the movie *MoneyBall*, Billy Beane, head coach for the Oakland Athletics baseball team, has a resource problem. He recruits good players, but when they're successful, other teams steal them away. With a limited budget, Beane decides to try a new approach. He hires players who have been rejected by other teams. He knows each player he recruits has strengths as well as a career-limiting flaw.

To build a willing team, he helps each person focus on their strengths and rely on others to compensate for their weaknesses. The results? His team won 19 games in a row, setting the world record for consecutive wins.

If you want to do more with less, help individuals play to their strengths and compensate for weaknesses.

4 Unique Strengths

With *Play to Your Strengths* games, you'll focus on four different strengths.

- Talents Strengths: innate talents, or what you do well.
- Attributes Strengths: your interpersonal style, or way of relating.
- Leadership Strengths: skills required to lead projects and people.
- Trust-building Strengths: behaviors that build greater trust.

Every game helps you develop one or more of these strengths.

Check out the following pages to learn more about these four strengths and why they are important. Or, go directly to the game section and get started!

1. *Talent Strengths*

Can you quickly rattle off your top five talents? Probably not; yet this is the *one thing* you must know to contribute value and advance your career. In my work with leaders and teams, I've discovered most people are blind to their talents.

Why? Because our talents are so easy and natural for us that we take them for granted. Our talents are so much a part of us, we don't give them a second thought.

For instance, one day a service man came to my house to check out the furnace. At the door, he noticed a bolt was missing from my mailbox. He said, "I hope you don't mind if I fix this. It will just take a minute." I was astonished. He fixed my mailbox even though that was not his goal. He is a fixer; that's his talent. And he assumed it was no big deal.

Everyone has talents. We are born with five to seven core talents we carry with us through childhood and into our career, family, community, and retirement. With so much at stake, I encourage you to discover your talents and make them the centerpiece of your work.

The games in this manual help you discover your own and appreciate others' talents. They help you build your team, set priorities, make decisions, and achieve results.

Learn more about your talents. Take our online
360 Talent Assessment and discover your top talents.

2. Attribute Strengths

Attributes are your style, or way of being. Your style might be intense, curious, or laid back.

Attributes support your talents and create your personal brand. Your brand is what you're known for. Two people can have the same talent but different attributes, and this impacts what they offer. For example, a calm planner delivers a different service than a persuasive planner.

Attributes are part of who you are, so it's easy to overdo them. If you're too quiet, you can be overlooked. If you're too determined, you might not know when to quit.

Being aware of your attributes helps you manage them. To succeed at work, it's important to recognize and manage personal attributes.

The activities in this manual will help you and fellow team members talk openly about personal attributes. You'll learn how your attributes add value, and ways to manage them for peak performance. Knowing your attributes will also help you create a personal brand.

I hope you enjoy learning about attributes and the unique value you bring.

3. Trust-Building Strengths

If people don't trust you, it doesn't matter how talented you are—they won't use your services.

Mistrust is costly. A Deming study estimates that organizations waste up to *half* their time dealing with trust issues. Building trust early in relationships is key, and repairing broken trust is essential.

It is the simple things that break trust. A colleague unwittingly insults us; we suspect a co-worker is gossiping about us; our boss takes credit for our work. Resentment brews. Months and even years go by, and still we remember our disappointment.

Don't let mistrust derail your progress.

Building trust can be daunting, but the activities in this manual help you succeed. You'll learn trust-building vocabulary and how to talk openly about tough issues. You'll identify actionable steps you can take to build trust.

Using the games in this manual, you'll discover building trust is easier than you imagined.

4. Leadership Strengths

Do you know the difference you're making? I hope so, because it's very important.

To lead projects and people well, you need a wide variety of leadership skills. Most leaders have some of these skills, but not all.

The Leadership Contribution deck highlights twenty-five core leadership skills.
Using the cards, you can solicit feedback on what your team or projects need to move forward. Team members can quickly identify strengths and areas that need attention. With this information, you can compensate for weaknesses and move forward.

The Leadership cards help you assess project needs, make collaborative decisions, identity the right resources, and improve leadership effectiveness. With this feedback you'll feel confident the actions you're taking are the right ones.

Use the Leadership games in this manual to help you and your team focus on what matters.

How it Works

Inside this manual, you'll find step-by-step instructions on how to use *Play to Your Strengths* games. Every game is designed to engage participants, improve communications, and build trust. These games are ideal for large groups, teams, and individuals. So let's get started.

Play to Your Strengths Games include four decks of cards. In one box are the Talent and Attribute decks; in the other box are the Trust and Contributions decks.

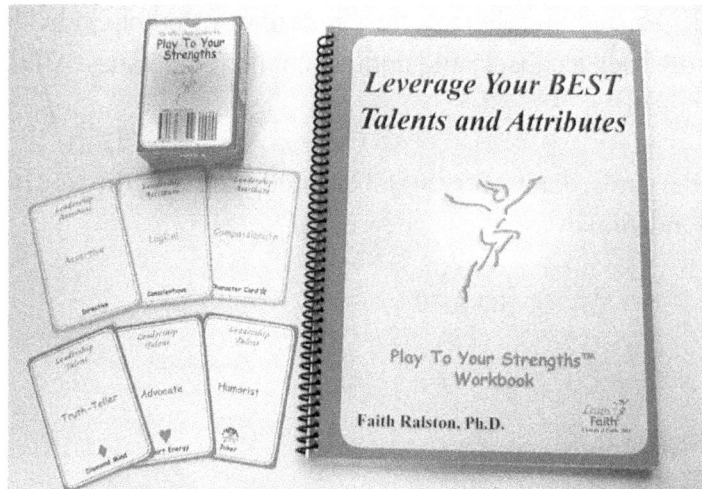

The purpose of each deck is unique.
Deck #1, the *red Talent deck,* helps participants discover and leverage individual talents.
Deck #2, the *orange Attribute deck,* helps participants strengthen style and communication.

Order Play to Your Strengths© card decks
for your team or group event.

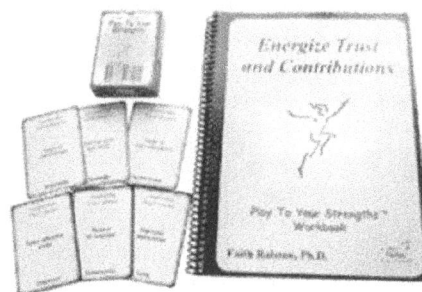

Deck #3, the *green Contribution deck,* helps people identify priorities and lead change.
Deck #4, the *purple Trust deck,* helps participants build trust and teamwork.

All decks can be used independently, or combined with other decks. There are different types of activities in this manual—some are quick and easy, while others take longer and go in-depth. If you are leading a workshop, it's easy to combine several activities and keep participants involved.

Why Use Cards?
Play to Your Strengths cards level the playing field. Everyone has a chance to contribute and share ideas. Using the cards opens up communication. Participation is stress-free, because participants don't have to rummage through their brains for answers.

The cards are versatile. You can use them in hundreds of ways to help individuals get acquainted, set priorities, build trust, seek feedback, and address challenging issues. All the cards are positive and help you move forward.

When working with the cards, don't worry about correctly defining the words on the card. Simply accept the definition individuals ascribe to their card.

Overview of Games and Purpose

Start by focusing on your goal and what you want to achieve; then pick a game that supports your goal. You can start with any game. Here's an overview of the games and the purpose of each one.

GAME 1: GRAB BAG (10 MINUTES)
Purpose: Warm up
This game is an easy way to engage everyone. Use this activity to help individuals get acquainted.

GAME 2: TALENT SWAP (10 MINUTES)
Purpose: Focus on strengths.
This activity gets everyone up and moving. Use it to energize a group and highlight individual strengths.

GAME 3: PLAY TIME (45 MINUTES)
Purpose: Improve individual performance.
This is a great warm-up or team building activity. Use it to help individuals talk open about strengths.

GAME 4: TUNE UP (1 HOUR)
Purpose: Increase team effectiveness.
This activity is ideal for any team. Use it to identify team's strengths, gaps and actions to take.

GAME 5: PICK OR PASS (20 MINUTES)
Purpose: Highlight individual strengths.
In this fun activity, individuals discover work preferences. Use it to highlight team and individual strengths.

GAME 6: BRAND YOU (30 MINUTES)
Purpose: Share personal brand.
In this game, participants describe their partner's strengths. Use it to highlight diverse talents in a group.

GAME 7: POWER BOOST (20 MINUTES)
Purpose: Increase recognition.
This activity generates a lot of good will. Use it to encourage positive feedback and raise morale.

Game 8: Guess Who (30 minutes)

Purpose: Discover hidden strengths.

This activity helps individuals discover how others see their strengths. Use it to build a positive climate.

Game 9: Give and Take (30 minutes)

Purpose: Improve collaboration.

This activity breaks down silos. Use it to improve cross-functional teamwork and communication.

Game 10: Trust Me (45 minutes)

Purpose: Learn trust-building skills

This activity helps individuals build trust. Use it to learn trust-building skills and address tough issues.

Game 11: Go Power (1 hour)

Purpose: Enhance leadership effectiveness.

This powerful activity helps team members give each other positive feedback. Use it to build team spirit.

Game 12: Win Big (45 minutes)

Purpose: Increase respect and collaboration.

This game helps individuals leverage their success pattern and improve individual performance.

Game 13: Top This (30 minutes)

Purpose: Speed up decision-making.

This fast-moving activity facilitates decision-making. Use it to get everyone on the same page.

Game 14: Wow Them (1 hour)

Purpose: Improve stakeholder relationships.

This high-impact game helps teams improve key relationships with customers, employees, and partners.

Game 15: Let's Focus (45 minutes)

Purpose: Advance key initiatives.

In this energizing game, participants vote with their feet. Use it to help groups set priorities and implement change.

GAME 16: CRISS CROSS (1 HOUR 15 MINUTES)
Purpose: Improve cross-functional teamwork.
This engaging activity breaks down silos and improves collaboration. Use it to help teams achieve shared goals.

GAME 17: BULLS-EYE (30 MINUTES)
Purpose: Gain consensus.
This fun game encourages individuals to share their point of view. Use it to promote dialogue and consensus.

GAME 18: TRUST TALK (1 HOUR)
Purpose: Address trust issues.
This activity helps participants learn trust-building skills. Use it to take effective action and build trust.

GAME 19: SHOUT OUT (30 MINUTES)
Purpose: Share your value.
This engaging activity helps individuals toot their own horn. Use it to help individuals contribute value.

GAME 20: HOT SEAT (45 MINUTES)
Purpose: Practice peer coaching.
In this high-impact activity, peers help each other tackle a challenge. Use it to build trust and peer collaboration.

Game Instructions

Let's get started!

Game 1: Grab Bag (10 minutes)

Purpose: Warm up

This game is an easy way to engage everyone and generate excitement. Use this activity to help individuals get acquainted and encourage conversation.

Directions	Use the red Talent deck for this activity. Depending on the number of participants, use one or two decks. Place all cards face down on the table.
Steps	1. Ask participants to randomly choose two cards from this pile, without looking at the cards.
	2. Select the card that best describes you. Rate this card based on how well it describes you, from #1 (low) to #10 (high).
	3. Round robin: each person shows their card and shares how well it describes him or her.
Sample Discussion Questions	In the large group, invite individuals to share:
	• Who learned something new about someone in the group?
	• What did you learn that surprised you?
	• Who needs help with a talent someone else has?
Example	Individual draws the Translator card from the red Talent deck, and rates herself #10 as a Translator. She says, "This describes me well because I speak several different languages."
Action	Encourage individuals to share their talents in the upcoming week.

Game 2: Talent Swap (10 minutes)

Purpose: Focus on strengths.

This activity gets everyone up and moving. Individuals trade cards to get a better hand. Use it to energize a group and highlight individual strengths.

Directions	You can use the Talent or Contribution decks for this activity. Use one or two decks, based on the number of individuals in the group. Shuffle the cards randomly, and deal three cards to each person.
Steps	1. Say: "The goal of this activity is to end up with three cards you love." 2. Invite participants to swap cards with others in the room. Encourage them to get the best hand possible within two minutes. 3. Swap cards and enjoy the fun!
Sample Discussion Questions	In the large group, ask: • Who has a card they love? • Who is stuck with a card they don't want? • Who has a card they want to swap? • Who wants this card?
Example	A creative individual is holding the Monitor card. He doesn't like to monitor progress or programs, and wants to trade with someone who enjoys this activity.
Action	Say, "Every job includes tasks we like and dislike. To contribute our best, we need to work with others who have talents that complement our own. This week, identify someone who has a talent you lack. Tell this person why you value their talents."
Variations	Use the green Contribution or orange Attribute deck for this same activity.

Game 3: Play Time (45 minutes)

Purpose: Improve personal performance.

This game is a great warm-up activity or in-depth team builder Use it to help individuals talk open about strengths and weaknesses.

Directions   Give everyone a deck of red Talent cards.

Steps
1. Ask participants to sort their Talent cards into three relatively equal piles.
   - In the High pile, place talents you excel in.
   - In the Moderate pile, place talents you do relatively well.
   - In the Low pile, place talents you do poorly.
2. From the High pile, select three talent cards you enjoy using and do well. Reflect on your current job. Ask yourself, "Am I using these talents in my current job? How can I leverage these talents?"
3. From the Moderate pile, select one talent you would like to use more often. Ask yourself, "What is one Moderate talent that if I used it more, would help me a lot?"
4. From the Low pile, select one talent card you need in your role. Ask "How can I compensate for this low talent? What system, process, or person can help me in this area?"
5. Share with a partner.

Example
Discussion
Questions

Who learned something new about someone in the group?
   - What did you learn that surprised you?
   - Who needs a talent someone else has?

Example   Individuals share their High, Moderate and Low talents: "I am high in the Creative talent and have lots of ideas. However, I'm moderate in the Planning talent and want to get better at this. I am low in the Advocate talent, yet it's important to my success. So I want help in this area."

Action   Share one action you will take to maximize your talents.

Variations   Ask individuals to share only High and Moderate talents. Omit Low talents. Use the Attribute card deck for this same activity. The Attribute deck identifies strengths and gaps in your personal style.

Game 4: Tune Up (1 hour)

Purpose: Increase team effectiveness.

This activity is easy and ideal for any team. Participants identify the team's strengths, gaps and actions needed. Use it to accelerate team performance.

Directions   Give everyone a deck of red Talent cards. If you have four or more people, divide into subgroups of two or three people.

Steps
1. Ask individuals to silently sort their talent cards into three relatively equal piles to indicate what they perceive as their team's strengths and weaknesses.
    - In the High pile, place talent cards your team does well.
    - In the Moderate pile, place talent cards your team does moderately well.
    - In the Low pile, place talent cards your team is missing or does poorly.
2. Ask subgroups to share their cards and agree on three High talents, one Moderate talent, and one Low talent of the team.
3. Ask subgroups to identify examples for each talent selected, and why each is important for team success.
4. Invite subgroups to share their cards with the entire team. Note: Do this in three rounds. In the first round, share High talents and examples. In the next round, share Moderate talents and why each is important, and in the third round, share Low talents and the implications for the team due to their absence.
5. As a group, brainstorm actions the team can take to maximize High talents, increase Moderate talents, and compensate for Low talents.

Example   Use these questions to encourage dialogue and application:
Discussion   - What are our Top talents as a team?
Questions   - What have we achieved with these talents?
                   - What are our Moderate talents as a team?
                   - Why are these important?
                   - What actions can we take to increase these talents?
                   - What are our Low talents as a team?
                   - Are they critical to our success as a team?
                   - How can we compensate for our low talents?

Example   "Our team is High in the Analyzer talent. We can quickly assess the pros and cons of different options. We are moderately good Advocates, so we need to spend more time promoting our ideas. We are low in Innovation. Once a quarter, we will invite an outside facilitator to help us brainstorm innovative solutions."

Action   Agree on three actions the team will take. Be specific. Clarify when and how these actions will happen, and who is responsible.

Variations   Repeat this activity using other decks. Use the green Contribution deck to identify leadership strengths of your team. Use the Trust deck to identify trust-building strengths of the team. Use the Attribute deck to identify your team's personality and style strengths.

Game 5: Pick or Pass (20 minutes)

Purpose: Highlight individual strengths.
In this fun activity, individuals either pick or decline a card based on their work preferences. Others chime in. Use it to highlight team and individual strengths.

Directions	Break into small groups of three to six people. Use one deck for each group. You can use the Talent or Contribution decks for this activity.
Steps	1. Place the deck in the middle of the table. Ask each group to turn the top card of their deck face-side up, so everyone can see it.
	2. Going clockwise and taking turns, individuals can either pick up or decline the card. Others can encourage this person to pick up the card.
	3. If no one wants the card, it is placed in a None pile.
	4. Continue until all the cards are distributed among team members or placed in the None pile.
	5. When all the cards are distributed, invite individuals to share their favorite card.
Sample Discussion Questions	Discuss these questions as a group: • Based on the talents on this team, what kinds of projects can we do well? • What talents are we missing? Refer to the None pile. • Given our missing talents, what might we struggle with as a team? • Discuss implications. What other teams are you on? How might this learning apply?
Example	"Collectively, we have a lot of Deal-Maker talents in this group. We could really make things happen. However, we are low in the Coach talent, so we might not bring others along."
Action	Share one thing you learned from this activity.
Variations	Repeat this activity with a different deck.

Game 6: Brand You (30 minutes)

Purpose: Develop your personal brand.
In this game, participants introduce each other to the group and describe their partner's strengths. Use it to highlight the value of different styles.

Directions	Give each participant a deck of orange Attribute cards.
	Say, "Your attributes are your style, or way of being. Knowing your attributes helps you create your unique brand. This activity will help you identify your attributes and communicate the value you bring to projects and others."

Steps

1. Ask participants to sort Attribute cards into three relatively equal piles:
   - In the High pile, place attributes you use often and consistently.
   - In the Moderate pile, place attributes you use sometimes, but not routinely.
   - In the Low pile, place attributes you use rarely and inconsistently.
2. Reflect on your High attributes and answer these questions: "How do my top attributes help projects and others succeed? What do others appreciate about these attributes?"
3. Pair up, and share your top attributes with a partner.
4. In the large group, introduce your partner to the group. Share your partner's attributes, and how this person adds value.
5. Introduction: "This is (name), and his/her top attribute is ____. With this attribute, he or she adds value to projects and others in this way..."

Sample Discussion Questions

Discuss as a group:
   - How did it feel to be introduced?
   - What did you discover about your attributes?
   - What attributes do we have in common?
   - How do your attributes contribute value to projects and others?
   - Who has an attribute you wish you had?
   - Have you ever overused your best attribute?

Example

Introduction: "This is Jo Anne. Her top attribute is Confidence. Her confidence helps her tackle difficult projects. Also, it inspires others to get on board."

Action

Identify one situation that will benefit from your unique attributes. Share.

Variations

Repeat this same activity with a different deck.
Use the red Talent deck to share top talents. Use the green Contribution deck to share leadership strengths. Use the purple Trust deck to share high trust-building behaviors.

Game 7: Power Boost (20 minutes)

Purpose: Increase recognition and appreciation.

This activity generates a lot of good will. Participants give each other positive feedback, and everyone gets a turn. Use it to shine the light on individual abilities.

Directions   Give each person a deck of orange Attribute cards.

Steps
1. Ask individuals to select one attribute they appreciate about each person on the team.
2. Round 1: Choose one person to receive positive feedback from others.
3. Others share one positive attribute they selected for this person, and describe the impact of this behavior on the team.
4. Repeat until everyone has a turn.
5. Option for an intact team: Select one attribute card you want this person to demonstrate more often. Share how this will help you and projects succeed.

Sample Discussion Questions   Discuss as a group:
- How did it feel to receive feedback on your attributes?
- What surprised you?
- What did you learn?

Example   "I choose the attribute Precise to describe Jim. I appreciate this attribute in Jim, because he helps me avoid mistakes and be alert to details I might miss."

Action   Invite everyone to share one learning or action they will take.

Variations   You can use a different deck for this same activity.

Game 8: Guess Who (30 minutes)

Purpose: Discover hidden strengths.

This activity helps individuals discover strengths they might be taking for granted. Use it to build teamwork and foster a positive work climate.

Directions   Give every person a deck of Attribute cards.

Steps
1. From the deck, select three cards that describe your strengths. Hide these cards.
2. Choose one person to start the round (Person A). Note: Person A does not reveal his/her cards.
3. Others select one positive card from their own deck to describe Person A.
4. Going clockwise, individuals show their card to person A and say why they selected this card. All cards are positive.
5. Person A reveals his/her card only if it matches the card selected by others.
6. At the end of round, Person A shares his or her cards and any surprises.
7. Repeat with Person B.
8. Continue around the circle until everyone has a turn.

Sample Discussion Questions   Discuss these questions to debrief this activity:
- How well do others know you?
- What did you learn?
- What surprised you?
- What hidden strengths did you discover?
- How do your attributes help others?

Example   Person A shares: "I didn't realize others see me as compassionate. I'm glad to learn this about myself."

Action   Identify a situation where your attributes can help others. Share with the team.

Variations   You can use a different deck for this same activity.

Game 9: Give and Take (30 minutes)

Purpose: Improve collaboration.

This activity encourages groups to ask for what they want from each other. Use it to improve cross-functional relationships and two-way communication.

Directions	Use the green Contribution deck for this activity. Give a deck of cards to each person.
Steps	1. Ask individuals to sort their cards into High, Moderate and Low piles to indicate their strengths and weaknesses. Set aside the Moderate pile, as you will not use it for this activity.
	2. Now select three of your top strengths from the High pile. These are strengths you are willing to share with others.
	3. Next, select three cards from the Low pile. These cards indicate weakness, or areas where you need others to help you.
	4. Break into two equally-sized groups. Ask each group to stand on a different side of the room.
	5. Tell Group #1, "Take your three High cards and find someone in the other group who wants your help. When you find this person, ask: 'How can my talent be helpful to you?'"
	6. Reverse roles and repeat with Group #2.
	7. Tell Group #1, "Now take your three Low cards, and find someone in the other group to help you." Repeat for Group #2.
Sample Discussion Questions	Ask these questions to debrief this activity: • Who needed your help? • Who was willing to help you? • What kind of help did you give? • What kind of help did you receive? • How did it feel to offer help? To ask for help? • Is it easier to ask for help or to offer help?
Example	"Joseph can help me *Hold a steady course.*" "I can help Anne *Take a stand.*"
Action	Find someone to help this week, and ask someone to help you.
Variations	Repeat this activity using the Contribution or Trust deck.

Game 10: Trust Me (45 minutes)

Purpose: Improve trust among individuals.
This activity helps individuals and teams build trust. Use it to teach trust-building skills and address trust issues.

Directions   Give one deck of purple Trust cards to each person.

Steps
1. Ask participants to sort their Trust cards into three relatively equal piles:
   - In the High pile, place trust-building behaviors you use often and consistently.
   - In the Moderate pile, place trust-building behaviors you use sometimes but not routinely.
   - In the Low pile, place trust-building behaviors you use rarely and inconsistently.
2. Now go to the High pile, and select three trust-building behaviors. Which is most important?
3. Share a time you relied on your top trust-building behavior and experienced a positive outcome.
4. Go to the Moderate pile, and select one trust-building behavior you want to use more often.
5. Share the benefits of increasing this behavior.
6. Go to the Low pile, and select one trust-building behavior that is difficult for you.
7. Share the benefit of adding this trust-building behavior.

Sample
Discussion
Questions   Discuss these questions as a group:
- What are high trust-building behaviors you demonstrate often? Share examples and positive outcomes.
- What are moderate trust-building behaviors you want to increase? How will doing this more help you and others?
- What are your low trust-building behaviors? What happens because you are low in this area? What are the benefits of changing this?

Example   "I am high in this trust behavior: *Has Excellent Knowledge and Skills.* This helps me do my job well and instill confidence.

I am moderate in this trust behavior: *Listens Well.* To be a good leader, I need to be a better listener.

I am lowest in this trust behavior: *Resolves Difference of Opinion.* I tend to avoiding conflict. I want to get better at this and address issues before they derail our progress."

Action   Commit to one action you will take to improve trust.

Variations   Use the Contribution cards for this same activity.

Game 11: Go Power (1 hour)

Purpose: Enhance leadership effectiveness.
This powerful activity helps leaders improve communication and trust with their team. Use it to gain insights and improve leadership effectiveness.

Directions   Give one deck to each person. Use the red Talent deck, orange Attribute deck, or green Contribution deck for this activity.

Steps
1. The Leader asks the group for candid feedback on his/her strengths and weaknesses, and encourages individuals to share examples and make recommendations. The Leader may also ask a specific question, such as "I'd like your feedback on how well I delegate."
2. Instruct individuals to silently sort their cards into three piles of relatively equal size:
   - The High pile indicates the leader's top strengths.
   - The Moderate pile indicates the leader's average strengths.
   - The Low pile indicates the leader's low or missing strengths.
3. From the High pile, individuals select three cards that they believe are the leader's top strengths.
4. From the Moderate pile, individuals select one moderate strength they want the leader to demonstrate more.
5. From the Low pile, individuals select one card that will enhance this leader's success.
6. The Leader leaves the room while team is sorting their cards. While outside, the Leader also sorts the cards and selects three High strengths, one Moderate strength, and one Low strength for him or herself.
7. Once individuals have selected their cards, they move into small groups of two or three people.
8. Small groups discuss their cards and collectively agree on five cards:

   They identify the leader's top three strengths, one moderate-strength, and one low-strength. The group also generates examples and makes recommendations. When the group work is done, they invite the Leader to return.
9. Small groups take turns giving the leader feedback.

   Round #1. Small groups describe the leader's top strengths and how these competencies help the team and projects succeed.

   Round #2. Small groups describe a moderate strength they want the leader to demonstrate more. They give examples and describe the benefits of paying more attention to this area. They recommend actions to take.

Round #3. Small groups share one weakness the leader needs to manage in order to be effective. They recommend specific actions to compensate for this area.

10. At the end of this feedback, the leader shares his or her cards with the group. The leader thanks the group for their feedback, asks clarifying questions, and commits to actions he or she will take.

11. Leader invites participants to share what they learned from this process.

Sample
Discussion
Questions

Use these discussion questions in the small groups:
- What are the leader's strengths?
- What do you appreciate about these strengths?
- What are examples?
- How can leader leverage his/her strength?
- Ideally, what should the leader do more consistently?
- How will this help you, others, or projects succeed?
- What will be different as a result?
- What is a weakness for this leader?
- Why is this important to manage?
- What actions do you recommend?

Use these discussion questions in large group to share key learning:
- What did you learn?
- What was helpful to you?
- How can you support these changes?

Example

Example of feedback given to leader:

High Strength: You are great at helping us *Remove barriers*. This empowers us to get more done. Keep doing this. We appreciate it. (Leverage strengths)

Moderate Strength: We want you to help us *See the big picture.* Right now, we are operating in a vacuum. If you help us understand the customer and marketplace, we can make better decisions. (Do more)

Low Strength: We need you to *Help us build bridges to other areas.* Right now, other departments don't know what we do or why we exist. We recommend you schedule monthly meetings with department leaders. (Compensate or manage weakness)

Variations

You can use any combination of decks for this activity. However, I recommend you use only two decks. I often use the Talent and Attribute decks for this activity. However, the Contribution and Trust decks work equally well.

Game 12: Win Big (45 minutes)

Purpose: Increase respect and collaboration.

This game helps individuals identify their success pattern and share this awareness with others. Use it to improve individual performance and peer support.

Directions Give everyone a deck of red Talent cards.

Steps
1. Ask individuals to sort the Talent cards into three relatively equal piles:
   - In the High pile, place your top talents.
   - In the Moderate pile, place your average talents.
   - In the Low pile, place your low talents.
2. From your High pile, select your top five to seven talents. Set aside the rest of cards in this pile. From these five High cards, select one card—your top talent. Be selective. Now place this talent in the center in front of you.
3. Arrange your other High talent cards around this top talent. Place cards to show the sequence of actions you take to achieve results. Be creative. Some of us have a circular pattern, others are linear. Once you lay this out, this is your success pattern.
4. Next, from the middle pile, choose one Moderate talent you want to use more often. Place this card in your success pattern to indicate where it will help you the most. To identify this talent, ask: "What talent, if I used it a little more, will help me a whole lot? And where in my success pattern is this talent most helpful?"
5. Finally, choose one Low talent that is essential to your success, but which you will never excel at. Place this talent in your success pattern to indicate where you need help.
6. In groups of three, describe your success pattern to others. First, share your top talent and what you enjoy about this activity. Next, describe the steps you take to achieve results. (For example, "First I do this...then I do this...") Then share the talent you want to use more (your Moderate talent) because it will help you a lot. Finally, share your Low talent, and where in your success pattern you need help from others.
7. Document and share your success pattern by taking a picture of the card spread with your camera or phone.

Individual Ask these questions to discover your success pattern:
Reflection
Questions
- What is your top talent? What do you enjoy doing?
- What are your other top talents?
- How do your talents work together?
- What moderate talent do you want to use more? How will this be helpful?
- What low talent do you need to manage? Why is this critical?
- Overall, what is helpful for others to know about your success pattern?

Optional questions on Attributes:
- What top attribute supports your success?
- How does it help you?
- What moderate attribute do you want to increase?
- How will this help you?
- What attribute are you missing?
- How can you compensate for this?

Example This is of Avon's success pattern.

Leadership Talent	Leadership Talent	Leadership Talent	Leadership Talent
Researcher	Champion	Truth-Teller	Facilitator
♦	♣	♦	♥
Diamond Mind	Club Power	Diamond Mind	Heart Space

Example of Success Pattern

Avon's top talent is Champion. She likes to champion new ideas. She is bored if she is not leading a new initiative. Avon starts by doing Research.

Once she confirms the idea is a good one, she begins to Champion it. Throughout the process, she challenges the status quo using her Truth-teller talent.

After the idea is adopted, she stays involved and uses her Facilitator talent to ensure success. Using this success pattern enables Avon to achieve optimum results.

Variations   Add Attribute cards to success pattern activity.

Directions for adding Attribute cards: Invite participants to sort their Attribute cards into High, Moderate and Low piles. Then select one High, one Moderate, and one Low Attribute from each pile.

Say; "Now incorporate these cards into your success pattern. Identify when your High attribute is helpful. Pinpoint where you need to use your Moderate attribute more. Clarify when you need to compensate for a Low attribute. Describe how attributes contribute to your success."

Game 13: Top This (30 minutes)

Purpose: Speed up decision-making.

If your team or group is struggling to make decisions, use this fun, fast-moving activity to gain agreement. You'll get everyone on the same page and moving forward very quickly.

Directions   Give everyone a deck of green Contribution cards.

Steps
1. Ask individuals to sort cards into three piles of cards to indicate how well the team is doing with a project or initiative:
   - High cards indicate strong process.
   - Moderate cards indicate average progress.
   - Low cards indicate a need for attention.
2. From the High pile, ask individuals to choose two Contribution cards that are essential for success and are being used well.
3. From the Moderate pile, choose two Contribution cards that need to increase for the project to succeed.
4. From the Low pile, choose two Contribution cards that need more attention for the project to succeed.

   Round #1. Share High cards first. Discuss: How are these contributions helping us move forward? *Note: Don't skip this step. It's important to recognize what's working and keep doing this.*

   Round #2. Share Moderate cards and discuss: How will doing more of this help the project succeed? What actions can we take to increase this contribution? Who are the best resources to help us?

   Round #3. Share Low cards and discuss: What is the consequence of being low in this Contribution? What is needed for the project to succeed? What actions can we take?
5. Finally, ask individuals to select three Contribution cards they are good at individually.
6. Ask, "Who has a Contribution that will advance this project? Who can help us *Define our vision?* or *Learn new ideas?*"
7. Summarize project priorities and follow up actions.

   Option: Repeat this activity using the Trust cards.

Example   Here is a sample team summary of this activity:
- High contribution: We are doing a great job of *Building bridges to other areas.*
- Moderate contribution: To succeed, we need to do a better job of *removing barriers.*
- Low contribution: We need to *Create innovative solutions* if we want to keep this customer.

Who can help:
- Jeff and Anne are good at *Creating innovative solutions.* Let's prioritize their time to focus on this.
- Our VP can help us *Remove barriers.* We need to enlist her help.

Variations   Use the purple Trust cards for this activity to identify actions needed to build greater trust.

Game 14: Wow Them (1 hour)

Purpose: Build stakeholder relationships.

This high-impact game helps teams build trust with different stakeholder groups. Use it to improve relationships with customers, employees, and strategic partners.

Directions   Before the session, identify three to five key stakeholders with whom you want to build greater trust. Invite participants who have knowledge and insight into these stakeholder groups.

Steps   1. Share your goals and why it's important to build trust with stakeholders. Then break into groups based on knowledge and interaction with different stakeholder groups.

2. In the small group: briefly share what you know about this stakeholder.

3. With the stakeholder in mind, sort the Trust cards into three piles:
   - High cards indicate you often demonstrate these trust-building behaviors with this stakeholder.
   - Moderate cards indicate you sometimes demonstrate these trust-building behaviors with this stakeholder.
   - Low cards indicate you rarely demonstrate these trust-building behaviors with this stakeholder.

4. Next, identify trust-building behaviors that will help you build a stronger relationship with this stakeholder. Say, "Given the relationship we want with this stakeholder, what behaviors do we need to demonstrate?"
   - From the High pile, select three trust-building behaviors you want to *continue doing.*
   - From the Moderate pile, select one or two trust-building behaviors that you want to *do more often and consistently.*
   - From the Low pile, select one or two trust-building behaviors you want to add or increase.

5. Individuals share the Trust cards they selected, and their rationale for selecting each one.

6. As a group, agree on the three most important behaviors you want to Continue (High pile), one or two that you need to Do More (Moderate pile), and one or two that you need to Add (Low pile).

7. In the large group, have small groups share the trust-building cards they selected. Ask each group to share their High cards first. In the next round, share Moderate cards, and in the final round, share Low cards. Ask for examples and implications.

8. Ask small groups to identify actions needed to improve trust with their stakeholder group.

9. In the large group, invite small groups to share their recommendations and action plan. Identify the strategies that apply to all stakeholder groups. Develop a master plan to address similar needs, such as "improve communications."
10. Develop a follow-up plan and commit to action.

Sample Discussion Questions

Use these questions to assess how well you are building trust with different stakeholders.

Identify high-trust behaviors.
- What trust-building behaviors are we demonstrating often?
- What are the benefits of continuing these behaviors?

Identify moderate-trust behaviors
- What trust-building behaviors need to increase? Why are these important?
- What are benefits of increasing these behaviors?

Identify low trust-building behaviors.
- What trust-building behaviors are low?
- What are the consequences?
- What needs to change?
- What recommendations do we have?

Develop action plan.
- What actions are needed to build trust with our stakeholder group?
- What is our plan of action?
- What will indicate we are making progress?

Tackle common issues.
- What issues cut across all stakeholder groups?
- What is our plan of action?
- Who is responsible?
- What will indicate we are making progress?

Example   We are High in this trust-building behavior: *Open to new ideas.* We listen and respond to customer suggestions. Action plan: Continue to keep our suggestion process alive.

We are Moderate in this trust building-behavior: *Hold a steady course.* Last month, we changed our policy three times. Customers want to know what they can expect. Action needed: We need to make fewer policy changes.

We are Low in this trust-building behavior: *Ensure no surprises.* Customers don't know what to expect. Action needed: We need to help customers anticipate changes.

Variations   Repeat this same activity using the Contribution cards.

Game 15: Let's Focus (45 minutes)

Purpose: Advance key initiatives.

In this stand-up game, participants vote with their feet. Use it to help a group set priorities and implement new initiatives.

Directions Start by formulating the question you want the group to answer. Ask: "What is needed to improve... (our strategy, product, leadership, teamwork, or culture?)"

Choose a deck that relates to your question. For instance, if you are asking "What skills do we need to advance this project," use the Talent and Attribute deck. If you are asking "What can leaders do to help us succeed," use the Trust and Contribution deck.

Steps
1. Use one deck. Deal out one card to each person until the cards are gone. If you have 50 people, everyone will receive one card. If you have 25 people, everyone will receive two cards. Don't worry if individuals do not have the same number of cards.
2. Invite participants to stand in a circle.
3. Ask your question. "Today we're going to assess the strengths and weakness of XYZ initiative. Look at the cards in your hand."
4. Say to participants, "Regarding this initiative, in which category do you believe your card falls?"
   - High: we are doing well.
   - Moderate: there is room for improvement.
   - Low: this project needs more of this.

   Now you are going to vote with your feet.
   - If you believe your card in High, step forward.
   - If you believe your card belongs in the Moderate category, stay where you are.
   - If you believe your card is in the Low category, take a step back.
5. Say, "Now look around. Based on where people are standing, what does this tell us?" Sample response: "We have more High cards than Low ones. We are doing well." Or, "We have mostly Low cards. This project needs attention."
6. Break into groups of High, Moderate, and Low raters.

7. Invite individuals to find a partner in their group and share cards. Describe why you believe your card is High, Moderate, or Low.

> High cards: Ask participants holding High cards to select three High cards. Be ready to share examples and state why these are important to continue.
>
> Moderate cards: Ask participants holding Moderate cards to select two cards that if improved, will accelerate the project's success. Be ready to give examples and recommend actions needed.
>
> Low cards: Ask participants holding Low cards to select two cards that require attention or the project will be at risk. Be ready to share examples and recommend actions needed.

8. Invite small groups to report results to the large group. As a group, agree on actions needed and create a follow-up plan to ensure results.

Sample Discussion Questions

Ask these questions to encourage dialogue:
- What patterns do you see?
- On a scale of 1 (poor) to 5 (great), how accurate is this picture?
- What are we doing well?
- What are examples of this?
- What more is needed?
- How will this help?
- What needs to be improved?
- What are the consequences of this?
- What actions do you recommend?

Example

Participants rate progress on new initiative:

High: We are Confident. We set a vision and we're moving confidently towards it.

Moderate: We are average Orchestrators. We try to do everything at once. We need to prioritize and focus on actions needed.

Low: We are low in Coaching. We need to give our partners better guidance and support.

Variations

You can use any deck for this activity. Repeat the same activity for a different initiative.

Game 16: Criss-Cross (1 hour 15 minutes)

Purpose: Improve cross-functional teamwork.

This engaging activity breaks down silos and improves communication. Use it to facilitate two-way communication and achieve shared goals.

Directions   Use this activity with two or more teams. Ask participants to stay with their team. Give one deck of green Contribution cards to each person.

Steps
1. "Our goal today is to improve communication and teamwork across functional boundaries. You will give feedback to each team present, starting with the team on your left."
2. Individually sort your cards into three piles:
   - In the High pile, place cards the team to your left performs well.
   - In the Moderate pile, place cards this team needs to do more.
   - In the Low pile, place cards this team needs to improve.
3. Individually, select one High card that is a strength, choose one Moderate card you want this team to do more, and pick one Low card this team needs to manage better. Select cards for each team that is participating in this activity.
4. As a team, discuss the cards selected by individuals. Then narrow in and choose two High cards (Do well), one Moderate card (Do more) and one Low card (Manage better) for each team you are assessing.
5. Select one or two ambassadors from your team. The ambassadors' role is to visit the other teams and share your team's feedback.

The ambassador might say, "This is a Contribution your team does really well, and this is how it helps us succeed. This is a Contribution we want you to do more, and this is how this will help us. This is a Contribution we want you to manage better, and why it's important."

6. Ambassadors have two minutes to give feedback to each team. It's helpful to keep time and ring a bell at the end of each round.
7. When finished, ambassadors return to their home team. Team members share feedback they received from visiting ambassadors. They discuss feedback and identify actions to take.
8. Teams return to the large group and share key priorities and actions they will take. Encourage discussion.
9. Wrap up: individuals share one thing they will do differently.
10. Build on the positive. Follow up to ensure progress.

Sample
Discussion
Questions

Use these questions and invite the group to share:
- What does your team do well?
- How does this help other teams?
- What does your team want to do more?
- Why is this important?
- What does your team want to improve?
- What are the benefits of this change?
- From this session, what are common themes?
- What did you learn?
- What are you personally motivated to change?

Example

Ambassador shares this feedback with a team:

High card: "We rated you High in *Removing Barriers*. You are great problem solvers and remove barriers along the way. We count on you for this."

Moderate card: "We rated you as Moderate in *Acquiring Resources*. You try to do too much yourselves. There are resources available, but you need to look up and ask for help."

Low: "We rated you Low in *Learning from Mistakes*. You keep solving the same problems over and over. Spend more time figuring out root causes."

Variations

Use any deck for this activity.

Game 17: Bulls Eye (30 minutes)

Purpose: Gain consensus.

This is a fun, competitive game that encourages individuals to share their point of view. Use it to promote dialogue and gain commitment.

Directions   Identify a challenge and formulate a question. Typical question: "How can we improve customer service?" (Or sales results, or work culture.) Use one Contribution deck for this activity.

Steps

1. Draw or tape a circle in the middle of the room. Make sure the circle is big enough for three people to stand comfortably inside it.
2. Invite participants to stand on the outside of the circle. Pass out two cards to each person.
3. Say, "Look at your cards. Do you have a Mission-Critical card we must do to improve customer service?"
4. Invite participants to briefly confer with two people and decide if they have a Mission Critical card.
5. Say, "There is room in the circle for three individuals who have a Mission-Critical card. Step forward now if you have one. There is only room for three people, so get here fast!"
6. Three people step into the circle. Invite each one to briefly share why their card is Mission Critical.
7. Ask the larger group, "Are these the most Mission-Critical actions we can take?" Invite individuals outside the circle to confer. At the end of one minute, say, "Who has a card that trumps one of these Mission-Critical cards in the center? If so, step forward, tap the individual on the shoulder and take their place."
8. Ask the challenger(s) to say why their card is more Mission Critical.
9. Repeat. Allow time for participants to confer with each other between rounds.
10. "Now we are going to widen the circle. Everyone who believes they are holding a Mission-Critical card, please come to the center now."
11. Allow free movement for two or three minutes. Anyone outside the circle can challenge a person inside, and say why their card is a higher priority. If the challenger persuades the person in the center to agree, the challenger takes their place in the circle. If the person in the center disagrees with the challenger, he or she retains their place in the circle.
12. Continue until there is majority support for three to five Mission-Critical actions in the center.
13. Break into small groups and brainstorm ways to achieve these three Mission-Critical actions.
14. Develop and commit to an action plan.

Sample Discussion Questions	Ask these questions to share your experience: • What do you believe is a Mission-Critical priority? • Why is this important? • Who wants to challenge this? • Why is your action important? • Who has an even higher priority? • Do we have agreement? • What are our top priorities? • How will we achieve them?
Example	Individual in the center says, "My Mission-Critical action is: *Help us understand why change is needed.* If we don't do this, we won't have buy-in or commitment." Challenger says, "My Mission-Critical action is, *Help us bridges to other areas.* We must break down silos to achieve our goal."
Variations	Adapt number of rounds to achieve your goal. Continue and use the Trust cards for another round.

Game 18: Trust Talk (1 hour)

Purpose: Learn how to address trust issues.

This activity helps participants learn trust-building communication skills and put them into action.

Directions   Attach three flip-chart pages to the wall. Write one of these words on a page: High, Moderate, and Low.

Have a roll of masking tape ready.

Give everyone a deck of purple Trust cards.

Introduce activity: "Today, we're going to focus on trust and identify actions we can take to build greater trust."

Steps   1.   Invite participants to assess the team's trust-building behaviors by using the Trust cards. Reflect on the team and sort Trust Factor cards into three piles.

In the High pile, place cards that represent trust-building behaviors the team does well.

In the Moderate pile, place cards that represent trust-building behaviors the team can improve.

In the Low pile, place cards that represent trust-building behaviors the team does poorly.

2.   Ask individuals to choose three High cards the team does well, one Moderate card the team needs to improve, and one Low card the team needs to remedy.

3.   On the flipchart pages, ask participants to tape their cards on the page that corresponds to their rating of High, Moderate, or Low.

4.   Ask: "What are common themes? Do we have more cards in the High, Moderate or Low categories? What does this mean?"

5.   Break into three groups and give each group one of the flipchart pages with the Trust cards attached. Ask the groups to look closely at their page and group the Trust cards into the five categories listed on the bottom of each card.

6.   Share results of each flipchart.

High: The *Communication* trust factor is our highest rating. What this means to us is...

Moderate Group: The *Caring* trust factors needs attention. What this means to us is...

Low: The *Conflict Resolution* trust factor is low. What this means to us is...

Sample	Ask these questions to further the discussion:
Discussion	
Questions	What are our highest Trust Factors?

Sample Discussion Questions

Ask these questions to further the discussion:

What are our highest Trust Factors?
- What are we doing right?
- How is this helping us succeed?

What moderate Trust Factor do we want to increase?
- How will this help us?
- What is consequence of status quo?
- What actions can we take?

What low Trust Factor do we want to fix?
- Why is this important?
- What is the consequence of ignoring this?
- What actions can we take?

Develop action plan:
- How committed are we to building greater trust?
- What are the benefits?
- What actions will we take?
- What will indicate we are making progress?
- What action will you take?

Example

The Leader invites the team to discuss themes.

"As a team, we are High in *Communication*. We readily share information, listen well, and seek to understand what's needed. Consequently, team meetings are engaging and useful."

"We are Moderate in *Caring*. Outside our meetings, we don't rely on each other. We need to do a better job of expressing appreciation and staying in touch."

"We are Low in *Conflict Resolution*. We don't resolve differences of opinions or address tough issues, so we have elephants in the room. This is slowing down our progress."

Game 19: Shout Out (30 minutes)

Purpose: Share your value.

This engaging activity helps individuals toot their own horn. Use it to help individuals articulate the value they bring to project and others.

Directions   Give each participant one red Talent deck and one orange Attribute deck.

Steps

1. Ask participants to reflect on their strengths and sort the red Talent cards into three piles:
   - Cards in the High pile indicate your strongest talents.
   - Cards in the Moderate pile indicate your average talents.
   - Cards in the Low pile indicate your low talents.
2. From the High pile, select one top talent. Choose the talent you enjoy most and are best at.
3. Next, sort the Attribute cards into three piles:
   - High: attributes in the high pile are most like you.
   - Moderate: attributes in the moderate pile are somewhat like you.
   - Low: attributes in the low pile are unlike you.
4. From the High pile, choose one Attribute card that is most representative of you.
5. Now place theses two cards side by side: your top Attribute card is on the left, and your top Talent card is on the right.
6. Working alone, complete the following value statement.
   I am a _____ (insert top Attribute) _____ (insert top Talent).
   Call me when _____ (identify problems or opportunities you like to tackle).
   I can help you achieve _____ (describe outcomes and benefits you can achieve).
7. Once participants have a first draft, form small groups. Instruct groups to help each other write a compelling value statement.
8. In the large group, ask individuals to share their value statements. Encourage eye contact when sharing. Discourage reading the statements. Encourage applause.
9. Reinforce the value of sharing your expertise. Say, "If you don't tell us, we don't know." Invite participants to reveal how it feels to share their strengths and learn others' strengths. Thank individuals for sharing.

Sample
Discussion
Questions

Ask these questions to help participants see where different skills are needed.
- Who can help us launch new projects?
- Who can help us be a high-performing team?
- Who can help us advocate for change.
- Who needs this person's expertise?
- What situations require this person's expertise?

Example

Individual shares value statement with the group:
"I am an *Assertive Champion* (person's attribute and talent). Call me when you are launching a new product and need a champion. I can help you get your project off the ground and generate enthusiasm for your idea."

Game 20: Coach Me (45 minutes)

Purpose: Promote peer coaching.
In this high-impact activity, peers help each other tackle a challenge. Everyone gets a turn to give and receive coaching. Use it to build trust and peer collaboration.

Directions   Give each participant a deck of red Talent and orange Attribute cards.

Steps   Introduce the activity. "Today, we're going to help each other deal with a challenge."

1. Ask participants to identify a challenge they would like to address.
2. Form small groups of three to four people.
3. The first individual briefly describes his or her challenge and invites peers to offer coaching advice. Then he or she leaves the room. *HINT: Don't worry if someone in the group doesn't know this person well. I've discovered the feedback of complete strangers is valuable and insightful.*
4. With the individual in mind, peers sort their cards into three piles:
   - High: cards that are this person's strengths.
   - Moderate: cards that are average strengths for this person.
   - Low: cards that indicate this person's low strengths.
5. Next, peer coaches reflect on the individual's challenge and choose five cards:
   - Select three cards from the High pile that will help the individual tackle their challenge.
   - Select one card from the Moderate pile that the individual needs to do more of to address his or her challenge.
   - Select one card from the Low pile the individual needs to address the challenge.
6. Invite the individual to return to the group.
7. Peers share feedback and offer coaching advice. Coaching begins with feedback on individual's strengths. Then peers suggest ways to increase moderate strengths and compensate for low strengths. All feedback is aimed at helping the individual deal with his or her challenge.
8. The individual shares insights and actions she or he will take, and thanks the group for their advice.
9. Repeat with the next person, until everyone in the group receives peer coaching.
10. In the large group, invite everyone to share what they gained from this activity.

Sample
Discussion
Questions

Use these questions to reflect on peer-coaching experience.
- How did it feel to receive peer coaching?
- How did it feel to offer peer coaching?
- What surprised you?
- What insights did you gain?
- What actions will you take?
- How can we continue to help each other?

Example

Here is example of peer feedback and coaching for individual who is struggling to gain commitment to a visionary idea.

"You are high in Analyzer Talent. Use this ability more to assess if this idea is what your customers really need."
You are moderate in the Visionary Talent. Share what you're doing, so others know where you're heading and can support you."
You are low in the Advocate Talent, so find a champion to help promote your ideas."

Variations

Use any deck for this same activity.

Your Turn!

I hope you have learned a lot and had a ton of fun. Hopefully you've gained valuable ideas to advance your career, build teamwork, and further strategic initiatives.

Now it's your turn. I invite you to create new games, find innovative ways to use *Play to Your Strengths®* cards, and keep the energy and learning high! Please share so others can partake, enjoy, and learn something new.

I'd love to hear about your progress and results, and I'm always here to help you achieve great results. Let me know how you are doing—email me at faith@faithralston.com so I can learn and celebrate with you.

Blessings!

Faith Ralston

About Faith

Faith Ralston is a popular speaker and leadership consultant. She is the CEO of Play to Your Strengths Consulting.

Faith is the author of *Play Your Best Hand* and the creator of the *Play to your Strengths Talent System for Leaders and Teams.*

Faith helps leaders build trust and teamwork needed to achieve their vision.

She has four grown sons and lives in Minneapolis, Minnesota.

Focus on Talents

PLAY YOUR BEST HAND

Faith's book helps you tap into talents — and achieve amazing results.

http://www.FaithRalston.com

Visit my website for practical strategies to leverage talents, empower your team, build trust — and achieve better results.

Take the Talent Assessment and discover your talents. Identify the talents of everyone on your team.

TalentQuiz.com

Leaders — Are you doing what you do best? Are you engaging employees and leveraging their best talents?

Leaders who help employees leverage their talents achieve better performance and results.

Learn more about your talents and the talents of everyone on your team. Take the online Talent Assessment and discover if your talent is:

- **DIAMOND INNOVATOR** — thinks outside the box and imagines what's possible.
- **HEART MOTIVATOR** — brings people together and build relationships.
- **CLUB ACTIVATOR** —sets new initiatives up for success.
- **SPADE IMPLEMENTER:** manages details and ensures projects are on time and within budget.

Leaders — are the individuals on your team fully engaged and committed to your goals?

Don't settle for less! It's the simple things that derail progress — poor communication, turf issues, conflicting priorities, and mistrust. *Play to Your Strengths Games* helps you tackle these issues directly and accelerate results.

Easy, interactive games help individuals get to know each other, discover their talents, and work as a team. Four distinctive card decks empower participants to talk openly, give candid feedback, and make shared decisions. Every game you play strengthens teamwork, trust, and communication.

Whether you are launching a new team or developing an existing one, *Play to Your Strengths Games* will transform your team into a powerhouse of performance. Plus, you'll have fun every time you play.

In this day of talent shortages, Faith Ralston gives leaders at every level some practical tips and tools to engage, develop and retain their precious human resources.
Jill Konrath, Chief Sales Officer, Author of Agile Selling

Faith's engaging activities helped us to successfully blend two different cultures and achieve integration faster.
CEO, Garry Bye, Client at East Central Energy

Play to Your Strengths Games casts familiar, tired issues in new and tempting ways that give participants insight and energy!
Carol Truesdell, Individual participant

What an enlightening advantage this process yields! The feedback comes in all positives and I learned specific actions I can take to improve my effectiveness.
Bob Cummins, Leadership Coach